From Chaos to Calm

How to Shift Unhealthy Stress Patterns and
Create Your Ideal Balance in Life

Gini Grey

Bloomington, IN Milton Keynes, UK

authorHOUSE™

AuthorHouse™
1663 Liberty Drive, Suite 200
Bloomington, IN 47403
www.authorhouse.com
Phone: 1-800-839-8640

AuthorHouse™ UK Ltd.
500 Avebury Boulevard
Central Milton Keynes, MK9 2BE
www.authorhouse.co.uk
Phone: 08001974150

First published by AuthorHouse 4/28/2006

ISBN: 1-4259-2933-8 (sc)

Library of Congress Control Number: 2006903499

Printed in the United States of America
Bloomington, Indiana

This book is printed on acid-free paper.

Cover Art copyright © 2006 Titania Michniewicz www.titania.ca

Dedicated to the Source within us all.

Contents

Introduction

"If we do not change our direction, we are likely to end up in the direction we are headed."

Chinese Proverb

We all want more balance in life, and yet stress and chaos have become the norm in our society. If we don't complain of being pressured, overwhelmed and stretched to the max, people think there's something wrong with us. Or they figure we're just lazy louts living the easy life. What's wrong with having an easy life? Can't we have a full, interesting and rewarding life without it being overly busy, hard or chaotic? I know we can, because I've spent several years exploring ways to let go of excess stress and create balance, while pursuing my passions and interests at the same time.

My discoveries into this topic began when I was working for a mental health organization, educating the public about mental illness. Over time I became more interested how to create and maintain wellness. I studied the various aspects of unhealthy stress; what causes it, how it affects people, ways to cope with it, and most importantly, how to avoid it. I designed workshops for corporate employees on managing stress and thought I had it covered pretty well. Until one day when I was so burned-out my doctor advised me to take a stress leave from work. What a joke, the supposed stress expert on stress leave! At that point I started to understand stress and balance on a deeper level. I had been practicing my teachings of getting adequate exercise and nutrition, practicing relaxations techniques, and adjusting my perceptions and attitudes towards stressful situations, but in the end all this did was buffer the effects of the stress. The underlying stress patterns continued to play out despite my healthy habits. It was then I realized that all of the traditional stress management techniques, as helpful as they were at relieving my symptoms temporarily, did not stop me from creating or attracting the circumstances, situations and people that caused the stress in the first place.

Once I recuperated from my burnout I began studying wellness from a broader holistic perspective. But my best learning came from applying all of the principles I learned into my life on a daily basis. It was then I started my own business, Celebrate YourSelf, designing and facilitating experiential workshops on the subject of creating balance. Over time I began to work with individual clients and now I want to reach as many people as possible guiding them to use these powerful tools to create ongoing balance and ease in their life.

I have written this book in a guided exercise format, much like being in a workshop or coaching session, to help you become aware of what your own ideal balance looks and feels like, what gets in the way of creating this, and how to shift unhealthy stress reactions and patterns so you can create ongoing balance in your life. It does not contain a recipe of the traditional techniques for coping with stress or dealing with the symptoms of stress. As useful as these techniques are, they have been covered in dozens of other books. The purpose of this book is to help you transform your life from the inside out, not the other way around.

The people who really need this book are the ones who will say they are too busy to read it, let alone do the exercises. If you are one of those people, I encourage you to think about how your life will be 5 years down the road if you continue at the same pace you are going. What regrets will you have? Will you wish you had taken the time back then to focus on your health and wellness? If we continue in the same direction, we'll end up with the same results. Change in our external lives requires making changes in our internal selves. It's one thing to have an intellectual understanding of stress and balance; it's another to have an experiential knowing. Putting aside half an hour a week, to read a chapter and do a few exercises will have a deep and lasting impact on your life, and on the lives around you.

When we let go of stressful patterns and find our own unique state of balance, we free up our energy to pursue greater passions in life. We discover what's truly meaningful to us and are inspired to create our lives from a place of calm instead of chaos. Rather than feeling like life is drudgery or frustrating, our lives become peaceful, rewarding and extremely satisfying. We open up to our inner joy and can't help but spread this to others in our life. So if you're ready to shift your current state of balance, grab a pen and a pad of paper and let's begin.

Balance

"Go confidently in the direction of your dreams. Live the life you've imagined."

Henry David Thoreau

It's the norm to feel out of balance these days, with so much going on in the world. People seem to be getting busier and busier and more and more stressed as time goes on. We all know the effects this has on our mental, physical, emotional and spiritual health. But what about the impact this has on our relationships, families, businesses and communities? And yet, we still get hooked in to filling our days with more tasks than there's time for. Have we become a society of busyaholics addicted to the rush of being stressed?

It would be easy to blame our stress and imbalance on the rise of technology, the change in family structures, or chaotic world events. But does blaming the social infrastructure make us feel any better, healthier or more balanced? No, and neither does pointing a finger at our boss, our workload, our spouse or our kids. At some point we have to look more closely at ourselves, the choices we have made and the decisions we are making in the moment if we want to change the direction we are going. No one has forced us into our lifestyle. No one else controls our thoughts or our reactions. And the only person responsible for bringing our life back into balance is us.

Wouldn't it be great if we could just hire someone to wave their magic wand and transform our lives into our ideal vision of balance? Ah, yes it would, but in reality if that were possible, it wouldn't take long before we'd turn our lives back into chaos again. Why? Because we are hardwired for effort and struggle. In the old days our relatives' survival depended on hard work and making it through tough times. In the even older days our ancestors' survival depended on a fight or flight reaction. What once worked and was coded into our DNA is now unnecessary in most situations and deadly in others. But without changing this programming within ourselves, we resort back to our old habits.

We know in our heart of hearts that it is time for something new; a new way of doing and a new way of being. We also know that this means changing from the inside out because most of us have tried to change everything in our outer lives only to end up with the same chaos over and over again. In order to make this internal shift, we need to take time to notice what's going on for us mentally, emotionally, physically and behaviorally. This can be difficult because we've been conditioned to be doing, doing, doing, focusing outside of ourselves, and the moment we stop we feel guilty, lazy and unworthy. This then triggers us back into our old behaviors. So if we want to create permanent change, we have to dig deeper into our habits and patterns and begin to alter them one by one.

First we need to discover what our current state of balance is. Then we need to become aware of what our ideal state of balance is so we can chart a course in this direction. What do I need in order to feel whole and healthy? How would my day flow? What would my attitude be? How would I respond to life's ups and downs if I were maintaining and ideal balance? This might include detaching from judgments, unrealistic thinking patterns and dysfunctional behaviors. It will also most likely involve weeding out limiting beliefs and creating a new structure of supportive beliefs to work with. Overall it means taking the wheel of control from our egos and putting it back into the hands of ourselves. Our true Selves. Our authentic Selves. Our spiritual Selves, higher Selves, evolved Selves, or whatever you want to call that timeless, eternal and powerful core essence that we are. From here we operate from an internal balance which is automatically reflected onto our external world.

We have the power to change our life patterns, one piece at a time. Can you imagine the ripple effect our new found balance will have on our relationships, families, businesses and the world?

Chapter 1

Exploring Your Ideal Balance

Balance is unique to each of us. My idea of balance might be completely different from yours. For me, I need a lot of slow peaceful moments, walks in nature, and stretches on the couch to cushion the more excited burst of energy, ideas, writing, teaching, coaching, counseling, learning and socializing I often like to do. I've become aware of the natural rhythms of my body and try to support these while honoring my creative and expansive aspects at the same time. Not always an easy feat, as my body has comfort as its top priority, while my mind has active learning and teaching on the top of its list, and the deeper eternal me just wants to experience as much of life as possible. Perhaps I could find a way to teach an online course using my laptop while resting on an inflatable couch that is twisting down a white water river. So what could you be doing more of or less of to create your ideal balance in life?

When our lives truly are in balance we feel peaceful, energized, and fulfilled. When our lives are out of balance we can feel hurried, bored or overwhelmed. For some the teeter-totter swings to a lack of stimulation or feeling bored or blocked, but for many it swings to over-activity, busyness, or feeling pressured. Oscillating between the two becomes like a roller coaster ride until one day you discover you're just coasting along from one bottoming out experience to the next. That's when most people are finally ready to get off the ride and find a new way of living. Fortunately none of us has to wait that long if we don't want to, we can get off and choose a new path anytime. One that supports us rather than depletes us.

There are many ways to look at balance in life. We can see how much time we are spending in the various aspects of our lives; work, exercise, family, social, chores, personal growth and so on and see if it appears balanced or not. We each have a different idea of what is best for us. Then it's a matter of adjusting our schedules to keep it in balance. Another way is to look at mental, physical, emotional and spiritual aspects of ourselves to see if we feel healthy in each of those areas. What about time spent with others versus time spent alone? Depending on whether we are more introverted or extraverted will determine how much socializing or down time we need. It also may depend on the time of year. Many people's rhythms follow the seasons, requiring more rest and alone time in the winter, more creativity in the spring, more recreation in the summer and so on. And many of us have our own seasons of needing to cocoon, grow, flower, or let go no matter what time of year it is. There is also balancing the right and left sides of the brain with time for logical, thinking projects and time for creative, insightful activities. It's really about knowing what's best for us. No one else can tell us this, and even if they could, would we listen?

What is your current state of balance? Following are a few tools for discovering your overall levels of balance. Having this awareness is a great starting point for creating your ideal balance in life.

Exercises for Assessing Balance

Wheel Of Life

The Wheel of Life exercise is a tool used by many personal and professional coaches in helping clients asses their current levels of satisfaction in various aspects of their lives. To do this, first decide how many areas of your life you want to look at. The most common areas include; career, finances, health, romance/ significant other, fun/social, exercise, friends/family, and personal/ spiritual growth. Then draw a large circle on a sheet of paper and divide it into the number of areas you are assessing. It will end up looking like a pie chart. Label each section of the pie with one of your areas. Rate each area on a scale of 0 to 10, with 0 being at the center of circle and representing no satisfaction and 10 at the outer edge of the circle indicating complete satisfaction. Draw a line across the section of pie to show your level of satisfaction in each area. Once all areas have been completed, look at the wheel to see how balanced it would be if you were to roll it down the street.

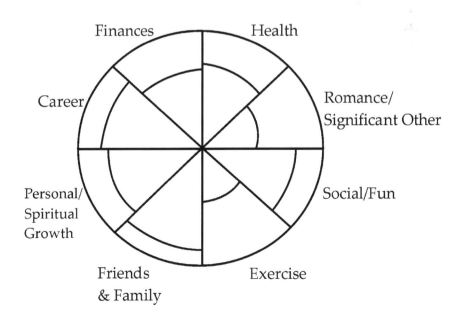

If it looks fairly bumpy like the example above, reflect over each area to see what actions you can take to restore it back to balance. Choose three things could you do this week to create more balance in your life.

Balance Quiz

This is a quiz I created to help people identify the mental, physical, emotional, spiritual and social levels of balance they currently are experiencing.

Circle the number that indicates how you would rate your current level of satisfaction in each category using the following scale:

Not good	Fair	Good	Really Good	Great
1	2	3	4	5

Physical

1. My eating habits and overall nutrition level   1 2 3 4 5
2. The amount of exercise I am getting   1 2 3 4 5
3. The time I spend relaxing & unwinding   1 2 3 4 5
4. Being in tune with what my body needs   1 2 3 4 5
5. How I feel about my overall health   1 2 3 4 5

Score for Physical Balance (total of all 5 numbers) =

Mental

1. Thinking positively about myself   1 2 3 4 5
2. Amount of intellectual stimulation   1 2 3 4 5
3. Ability to concentrate and focus   1 2 3 4 5
4. Attitude during stressful situations   1 2 3 4 5
5. Amount of silence with no mental chatter   1 2 3 4 5

Score for Mental Balance (total of all 5 numbers) =

Emotional

1. Being aware of my feelings/emotions   1 2 3 4 5
2. Expressing and releasing my emotions   1 2 3 4 5
3. Setting boundaries without guilt   1 2 3 4 5
4. Dealing with/releasing fears   1 2 3 4 5
5. Amount of laughter and amusement   1 2 3 4 5

    Score for Emotional Balance (total of all 5 numbers) =

Spiritual

1. Connecting to what's meaningful to me   1 2 3 4 5
2. Purpose and passion in my life   1 2 3 4 5
3. Expressing my creativity   1 2 3 4 5
4. Amount of peacefulness, ease and joy   1 2 3 4 5
5. Accessing my own wisdom and truth   1 2 3 4 5

    Score for Spiritual Balance (total of all 5 numbers)   =

Social

1. Enjoyable time spent with others   1 2 3 4 5
2. Connected to friends, family, community   1 2 3 4 5
3. Amount of time spent with/for myself   1 2 3 4 5
4. Participating in activities/hobbies I enjoy   1 2 3 4 5
5. Ability to communicate clearly and honestly 1 2 3 4 5

    Score for Social Balance (total of all 5 numbers)   =

At different times some areas of your life will be more balanced and some less balanced. To see how your overall balance is at this time in your life, take each category total and multiply by four to get a percentage out of 100. Then fill in the star points to see the bigger picture.

Score for physical balance: _____ x 4 = __ /100
Score for mental balance: _____ x 4 = __ /100
Score for emotional balance:_____ x 4 = __ /100
Score for spiritual balance: _____ x 4 = __ /100
Score for social balance: _____ x 4 = __ /100

At our core Inner Self we are always balanced so fill in the points of the star beginning at the outer edge of Inner Self as a base representing 0% balance and extend it to the end of the tips representing 100% balance. This will give you a visual image of how much balance you have in each area as well as a picture of your overall balance.

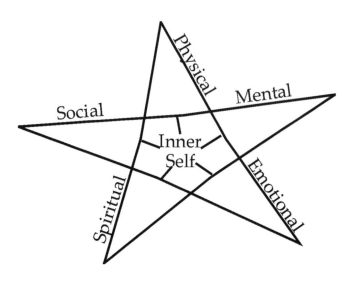

If you are not happy with the balance you have presently in your life, go back over each category to see where you would like to make a shift. Awareness is the first step in making positive change. Ask yourself what you can do to create the kind of balance you are looking for.

Needs

We each have certain needs that if unmet cause discomfort and certain values that if unexpressed lead to dissatisfaction in life. Discovering our needs and values is a wonderful way to explore the scales of balance in our life. Let's begin with needs. What do you need to have in your life to feel comfortable? Is comfort itself an important need: a cushy sofa to relax on, the comforts of home wherever you travel, soothing foods for your body? How about freedom; do you go stir crazy if you feel penned in? Or honesty; does it insult you when someone doesn't reveal their truth to you? Think about the various things that need to be met in your life on a regular basis. Write down any needs you are aware of. A way to test how important your needs are, is to imagine having your need met and then unmet. If you feel irritated by it not being met, chances are it is a priority for you.

Examples of not having needs met would be feeling upset when you don't feel accepted by others, or ticked off if people don't acknowledge or recognize you for your contributions, or being strongly triggered when people don't communicate clearly. Keep in mind that we all have these needs to some degree or another, but it becomes a strong motivating need when it is something that negatively impacts other areas of your life if it is not met. For me, if my desk and home are cluttered, it somehow boggles my mind and I can't be as creative as I'd like to be. It therefore negatively impacts my work and overall balance in life. Someone else might not be affected by clutter, but might have a strong need for clear communication and feel pre-occupied until they are able to speak their truth to someone they are having a conflict with.

Another way to determine your needs is by reading over the following list of needs to see which ones are important to you. When you think about what contributes to your peace of mind you might identify other needs not on the list. Make note of these as well. Once you have identified your main needs, rank your top eight needs starting with the most important, and then answer the questions below.

Acceptance	Relaxation	Freedom
Acknowledgment	Order	Loved
Recognition	Safety	Variety
Needed	Security	Kindness
Communication	Connection	Community
Clarity	Accomplishment	Aloneness
Honesty	Accuracy	Feelings

Comfort	Clarity	Encouragement
Quiet	Busy	Action
Peace	Control	Growth

★ Are you currently meeting your top eight needs? If not, why not?

★ How does meeting these needs affect your life? How does not meeting them affect your life?

★ How can you better meet your needs? Sometimes our needs are not being met because we are waiting for someone else to meet them. Ironically though, if we can not meet our own needs, say for love, acceptance or acknowledgment, we will not be able to receive these from others. Brainstorm a list of ideas on how you can meet any unmet needs yourself.

Values

Values are apparent in the way we express ourselves, live our life and follow our purpose. When we are not honoring our values, life doesn't seem as rewarding and fulfilling. Spend a few minutes contemplating what you value about your work, your friends, your community, and your life in general. For example, if you are not expressing your creativity, does life seem unrewarding? Do you get a huge satisfaction out of being a catalyst in peoples' lives? Is pursuing pleasure a top priority in your life?

Write down whatever values you are already aware of. Then look over the following list of values and reflect on what they mean to you. Choose your top eight values ranking them according to their importance, and then answer the questions below.

Adventure	Self-Expression	Planning
Discovery	Teaching	Sensuality
Learning	Winning	Risk
Spirituality	Power	Inspiration
Catalyst	Mastery	Ease

Contributing	Intuition	Fun
Service	Beauty	Compassion
Creativity	Pleasure	Leadership
Relatedness	Sensitivity	Imagination
Emotions	Partnership	Advocacy

★ Where in your life are you honoring your top eight values?

★ Which ones are not being honored and why?

★ What steps can you take to more fully honor your values?

Bringing Needs and Values Together

Meeting our needs is important if we want to be able to express our values fully. Reflect on the following questions.

★ Which of your needs must be met before you can move onto expressing your values?

★ Some needs go hand in hand in supporting values, while other needs are sometimes in conflict with certain values. Which of your needs and values go well together? Which needs and values conflict?

★ For any conflicting needs and values, how you can meet the need and honor the value at the same time?

Chapter 2

Creating Internal Balance

Once you've identified the various aspects of your life you'd like to bring into balance, it may take some sorting for it to all fall into line. But if trying to keep it all in balance feels like a full time job, what's the point? If balance were just about scheduling and time management it would be much easier than it ends up being for most people. This is because schedules don't always work. Things come up, plans change, interference's occur. Life is not rigid and static, it has an ebb and flow, and when we can go with this process, balance naturally ensues. I discovered this the long way, or as some would say, the hard way. But nevertheless it was the best way for me to learn as now I know it inside out and can lead others through the process in a quicker and easier way.

Years ago, I was considered a 'go getter'. Taking on responsible jobs, doing volunteer work, taking courses, and basically trying to run the world. I was also an excitement junkie; at first through my own adventures, and then by experiencing the thrills vicariously through other's chaos so I could play out my care-taking role and rescue them from their own disasters. Even though I learned how to set boundaries, delegate, get lots of sleep, exercise, eat healthy and create social connections, I still continued to over tax myself. I thrived on this lifestyle, or so I thought, so I was not aware of what was happening to me on a deeper level. What I discovered later was that my body was running on nervous energy, not a zest for life like I thought.

Eventually the buffers of what appeared to be a healthy lifestyle couldn't sustain my overall physical, mental, emotional and spiritual health anymore so I decreased my work to part-time for several months and then to no work for almost a year. I was seeing an Ayervedic doctor who could read the internal workings of my system through ancient and holistic health assessment techniques. He advised that I spend my mornings relaxing with herbal tea, meditation and yoga and my evenings with relaxing music. No evening classes, meetings or socializing. This was hard to get used to, and of course, brought up feelings of uselessness and worthlessness because I wasn't contributing to the world through work or volunteering anymore. After re-charging my batteries I went back to school studying Transpersonal Psychology with my focus on wellness counseling and body/mind consciousness. I was also studying energy awareness and healing techniques. All of this led me to a deeper awareness and discovery of the importance of starting with an inner balance.

You see, it's not just about how many activities we have going on in our life, or how much relaxation time we schedule in; if we're addicted to stress and chaos we will find a way to bring it back into our life. Drama can be created out of the smallest things and catastrophes can crop up in the calmest times. Changing our external circumstances doesn't shift our external reality; only by changing our internal reality can we affect our external circumstances. We can change jobs, trade in partners, move to a new city and feel like we're starting over again, only to have the same movie playing over and over again in our lives. Like the saying goes 'wherever you go, there you are'. We are the common denominator in our lives. When we change everything around us but keep coming back to the same old patterns we have more solid proof that we are the ones creating them. It's easy to blame others for our predicaments, but that is only giving our power away. Knowing that we've created the circumstances of our lives doesn't mean blaming ourselves either. It's not about whose fault it is. It doesn't help to beat ourselves up for doing it yet again. Awareness of our patterns is important and then letting them go and discovering new ways of thinking and being are the answer. Unfortunately, most of us need to experience a lot of pain before we are ready to give up our old ways. If we can allow the peace and calm of balance to be a motivator, then perhaps we can take the easier route.

True balance is an internal state. It emanates from within us spreading out into our lives. When we experience what our ideal balance feels like and set our intention to have this operating in our life, external circumstances will follow suit. But it takes place from the inside out, so our beliefs, thoughts, and feelings shift first and then the world begins to take a different shape. We start to attract people and situations that reflect our inner calm and we naturally stay away from chaotic situations and people. I'm amazed at how peaceful my life is now. At first I thought I would be bored without a soap opera lifestyle, but instead my life is full and rich. As Marianne Williamson said in her book, *A Return to Love*, 'we don't get rid of the drama in our lives, just the cheap drama'.

As we become more balanced within, everything without falls into place. And even when it doesn't, we're less affected by it. It's like being in the eye of a hurricane; upheaval can be swirling all around us, but when we are calm at our core, we don't get caught up in it, we just see it for what it is.

Exercise for Balance

Envisioning Balance

One of the best ways to move into a new way of life is to envision it in all its glory. Imagining our ideal state of balance motivates us to keep making the necessary shifts to get there. Letting go of the old, comfy way of handling situations isn't so daunting when we have a pot of gold beckoning us from the other side. Imagining it also makes it appear more real for our mind and feel more real for our body so it becomes easier to attain. Try the following guided imagery exercise.

★ Set aside 10 – 20 minutes of undisturbed time where you can relax, close your eyes and envision what your ideal state of balance would look like, feel like and be like. Start by taking in a few deep breaths, letting go of any tension in your body. Breathe into your belly, your diaphragm and then your lungs. Scan your body starting from your head and neck and go slowly all the way down to your feet breathing into any tight areas and releasing the tension on the out breath. Imagine a dot of clear gold in the center of your head and see it expand and fill your whole body with clear, light, gold energy. Allow your whole body and mind to feel relaxed and balanced. Notice what this feels like physically and emotionally. Notice how calm your mind and thoughts are. From this balanced state, let your imagination show you what your life looks like being in your ideal balance. Start with one day; imagine how your morning would go being in balance, and then the rest of the day and into the evening. Notice what activities you are doing. Notice how you interact with others. Notice how your body feels as you go through your day. Notice how you feel emotionally, mentally and spiritually as well. Then scan through a whole week, and then a month. See yourself six months down the road in total balance; what is your life like? Use all of your senses to imagine this: seeing, feeling, smelling, touching, and hearing. Notice your connection to people, nature, the universe or anything else important to you. Soak in all of the positive feelings and let them fill your whole body, down to every cell. Set the intention to create ongoing balance by asking yourself how many ways you can find to create this type of balance in your life from this day forward. Then bring your attention back to your body and the chair you are sitting in and slowly open your eyes.

★ Write down your vision of your ideal balance so you can refer to it often.

Doing this guided imagery exercise regularly will help keep you focused on creating balance in your life. Spending 15 – 20 minutes at the beginning of each week imagining this state will help you set your ongoing intention. Spending 5 minutes at the beginning of each day or on a break during the day will help you to set the tone for the day. By making balance a top priority in your life, you will be amazed at how external events fall into place to support this.

Chapter 3

Recognizing What Blocks Your Balance

We all say we want to live a balanced life, so what gets in the way? Our first response is usually to blame something external we feel we have no control over. "I just get so busy, I have so many things to do, who has time for balance", is a common one. When we look for more specifics we might say something like, "my boss just keeps giving me more work to do and no one else can do it and it has to get done". So then we put our state of balance into someone else's hands. 'When things slow down at work I'll have balance', or 'when the kids are grown up and out of the house I'll have balance', or 'when I get a new job I'll have balance', or 'when my spouse starts to help around the house I'll have balance', or 'when I have more money I'll have balance" and the list goes on.

What would it be like to let go of all these external reasons, no matter how plausible they seem, and just have balance right now? What would it be like to feel a state of balance inside, no matter what the circumstance? To have a pile of work staring at us on our desk, and to pause, breath in balance and breath out chaos and approach the day from an inner state of calm. What if we chose to bring the state of balance with us wherever we go and to whomever we meet? Who knows, our external lives might just start to fall into balance as well. Deep down we know that this is how life works, because the universal laws keep telling us that whatever we create within will be mirrored without. So let's stop trying to do it the other way around. Let's stop giving our power away to others and to circumstances. If we can become aware of how we block our own state of balance, we can easily shift that and create a smooth pathway.

Exercise on Recognizing Blocks to Balance

Discover Your Blocks

We each have our own wisdom and knowledge of everything we need to do for ourselves. As we become aware of this, we unleash the power to change our lives in any direction we want. Quieting our thoughts and turning inward for answers is the first step. Try this exercise.

Sit quietly with your eyes closed and find a still, calm place in the center of your head. Let your insight guide you to answer the following questions and allow the information to reveal itself in whatever form it arrives. You may see an image or symbol, you may hear words within you, or just sense the answer. Ask yourself:

★ What gets in the way of me having balance in my life?

★ What is my attachment to this block?

★ What do I need to do to move beyond this and create balance in my life?

Another way to explore these questions is to write them down one at a time on a piece of paper and then let your hand write down whatever answers come up for you. Without searching for answers, allow your insight and subconscious mind to reveal the information. It may not make sense at first, but after writing a few responses down you may find a valuable gem.

Chapter 4

Bringing Yourself Into Balance

When we are caught up in the current of chaos it's difficult to know what we need to do in order find a state of balance, even if it's just a temporary state lasting long enough to gain some helpful insight. It's as though we need someone to give us a shake, instruct us to breathe and point us in the right direction. Everything has momentum, including our lives and sometimes the only thing that stops us is hitting a brick wall. If we can notice the signposts en route, one that says "stop", or at least "yield", we can slow down and take a detour into a more favorable locale. Hopefully this book is your signpost, guiding you to a more peaceful path.

Deep within us we know what we need in order to re-balance. We just need to sit still long enough to discover it. For some, going out into nature helps to ground us and bring clarity. For others sitting in meditation is a powerful way to calm and center the mind and explore intuitive answers. But for those who don't feel they have time for long walks in nature or are too antsy to sit in meditation there are two easy tools to use to get "centered" and "grounded" immediately.

When we are "centered", we are aware of ourselves as a spiritual being in a body which has thoughts, beliefs, feelings and emotions. From this centered place we know we are bigger than our body and our mind, and that we have the power to create what we want in our life. When we are centered we are also accessing our whole brain rather than one half at a time. From a peaceful still place we can access our logical linear side or our creative intuitive processes, or combine them together. From this place we feel more neutral and are aware of our truth.

When we are grounded we feel more connected to our bodies and can more easily release emotions and tension held in the body. We feel planted on the earth and therefore have a deeper sense of safety and control. When we are both centered and grounded we can find stillness and gain further insight into what we need in order to move in the direction of creating balance.

Exercises for Creating Balance

Centering

To center easily, close your eyes and bring all of your awareness into the center of your head. The center is back from your forehead a few inches and down from the top of your head a couple of inches. Experiment with this by purposefully shifting your awareness to the front of your forehead and notice what that feels like, then come back to center. Move your focus to the back of your head and notice what that feels like, then come back to center. Now imagine being on top of your head and notice that. Go back to the center of your head and see if you can find a still peaceful place there.

Grounding

To be more grounded in your body, imagine a grounding cord that goes from the base of your spine all the way down to the center of the planet. Let this be as wide as your hips and have a constant flow downward. To get a better feel for this, imagine getting rid of your grounding so you are ungrounded, and walk around the room and notice how you feel. Then re-create a grounding cord to the center of the planet and notice how you feel walking around the room now.

Intuiting Balance

To discover intuitively what you can do for the various aspects of yourself to create more balance, try the following exercise.

★ Sit quietly with your eyes closed being grounded and centered. Take a few deep breaths to relax your body and mind. From the still, calm place in the center of your head, ask your body what it needs from you. You may get images of things such as exercising, taking a bath and so on, or you might feel sensations of something physical like having a massage, or you might just hear your thoughts telling you what you need. Once you have an answer from your body, ask your mind what it needs from you and notice what comes up. Then place your hand over your heart and ask your heart what it needs. To finish, ask yourself, as a being that is bigger than your body, thoughts and emotions, what you need at this time in your life.

★ Write these ideas down and decide what you are willing to commit to over the next week. You can do this exercise each week or even every day to discover what your current needs are. Promise yourself only the things you are willing and able to follow through on. Building trust within you is important for creating balance.

Stress Patterns

"A cloud does not know why it moves in just such a direction and at such speed. It feels an impulsion ... this is the place to go now. But the sky knows the reasons and the patterns behind all clouds, and you will know, too, when you lift yourself high enough to see beyond the horizons."

Richard Bach (Illusions)

We can begin to create more balance in our lives simply by setting our intention. The next step involves moving beyond any blocks that may hinder us from having this balance. These blocks often include our automatic reactions, which become patterns over time. We all have our favorites, which we learned as coping mechanisms growing up. We were smart little kids and discovered very early on which reactions got our needs met. For some it was yelling and screaming, for others pouting and whimpering, and for some, the silent treatment worked best. Whichever method we employed, it may have worked fine for us as children, but as adults it is having a boomerang effect. It no more helps us to create balance in our life than closing our eyes while driving helps us to get to our destination. The problem is we've been responding this way for so long it has created deep neural pathways in our brain so slipping into these habits is as comfortable as putting on our favorite pair of slippers, only it's less conscious.

If we want to shift these unhealthy reactions into healthier responses, we need to turn off the automatic pilot switch and notice what we're doing. How do I react when things get stressful? Am I the eye of the hurricane or do I get caught up in the storm? When I was an excitement junkie I would create stress in my life by taking on too many projects at once and then go into my habitual catastrophic reaction; "if I don't get all this work done, by today, my boss is going to think I'm totally incompetent! Then he's going to conspire to fire me!! Then I won't have any money and won't be able to pay my rent and I'll have to live on the streets and beg for food, and people might not feed me and I'll die!" It's

33

much more fun to see it in action than read about it, but I think you get the picture – my eyes would usually be bugging out, my face looking strained and I'd be moving and talking at 100 miles an hour. And this was only one of my typical reactions; I had several others to choose from on any given day. None of them helped me to get the work done any faster or easier or more efficiently, and none of them supported me in producing positive results without exhausting myself in the long run.

Why we continue to respond with these unproductive thoughts and behaviors boggles the mind until we see the overall picture. It's not just that they are hard wired into our response system; it's that there is a motive and payoff for them as well. When we look closely enough, we can see the logical pattern of these illogical reactions. For me, I was attached to excitement because as a child growing up I didn't have very many playmates and was bored to death, as the saying goes. To not have excitement in my life as an adult triggered the fear of boredom, this triggered the fear of death, which created the motivation for chaos. Add to that my need for approval, stemming from low self-esteem, which motivated me to take on extra work. The harder I worked and the more stressed I felt, the more strokes I received for being such a good, hard working employee who gave 150% to the organization. Not a bad payoff, or so it seemed, until I didn't have the energy left to keep up the pace and started to disappoint people, especially myself.

To start the process of revealing our stress patterns, it helps to know what triggers us in the first place. Then we can identify our specific reactions to these, and more importantly, discover tools to shift these reactions. If we are still repeating old patterns, then its time to dig a little further into the background of our wacky ways.

Chapter 5

Discovering Your Triggers

We each have certain buttons, that when pushed launch us into our typical stress reactions. Some of us are irritated by the daily glitches in life like traffic, appliances breaking down, interruptions at work, and so on. Others take those things in stride and don't get knocked off center until a bigger situation occurs like a major deadline, an accident, or a change in jobs or residence. No matter what it is that pushes our buttons, we becomes less easily triggered when see how the chain of events operates.

If we know that traffic jams test our patience and lead us to white knuckle the steering wheel with one hand and use the other to wave our one finger solute to neighboring vehicles, all the while increasing the redness in our face until our blood pressure explodes, we can use this information to make wiser and more conscious decisions next time. If it's possible, we can take a different route or travel at a different time. If we don't have that luxury then we can bring soothing music or a comedy tape to listen to which will calm us and help us to let go of trying to control the traffic. By bringing our awareness to the situation, we can clearly see whether we have any control over the event or not, or whether we only have control over our reactions to it. But first, it helps to look at what triggers us most easily.

Exercise on Discovering Your Triggers

Tracking the Stress Patterns

To identify what events, situations and people trigger you, how you are affected by these, and how much control you have over all of this, take out a sheet of paper and create the following four columns similar to the example below.

★ Title the first one 'Events' and list of all the events, people and situations that cause you to feel stressed. Start with the smaller daily stresses and then list the bigger stresses.

★ In the second column label it 'Effects', and for each activity, write down the effects you experience: how you feel emotionally, physically, mentally, and spiritually.

★ In the third column, label it 'Control', and write down a yes, no or partially for whether you feel in control of this event happening.

★ In the final column, title it "Influence' and write down what your influence is around this event. It could be anything from how you influence its occurrence, how you influence the positive or negative effects you experience through your reactions, or how you could influence things to be resolved.

Events	Effects	Control	Influence
Traffic	Frustrated, angry tightness in body, thinking negative thoughts	No control over traffic	Left late for work. My negative attitude doesn't help. Could leave earlier or try another route or practice breathing and listen to fun music instead of getting angry.
Finances	Fearful, worried, panicking, tired, not trusting	Yes to some degree	Didn't budget well. Could start to track spending and create a budget. Instead of dwelling on the negative I could think positively and brainstorm ideas on how to get out of debt and then take action on them.

★ Reflect over all of the events and their corresponding effects, amount of control, and influences, to look for any patterns emerging. Are you affected in the same way by each of the events or does it differ? Why do these events trigger you in the first place? How many events do you feel in control of? Does not having control cause you to feel more stressed? Is there a common denominator when you go over the 'Influence' column?

The more we can become aware of what situations and circumstances trigger us and see how we contribute to these, the quicker we will be able to address them. It may involve avoiding situations if possible, taking control when it's in our hands or letting go when it's not, and shifting our attitudes so we don't over react. Our attitudes are key of course, because that is the one thing we are in charge of, and it's our one saving grace when everything is tumbling around us.

Chapter 6

Identifying Your Reactions

When we dig under the surface of stressful events and situations we often find that it is our perceptions and reactions to life's events that cause us to feel stressed, more than the situation itself. It's our old coping mechanisms at work keeping us going down the same path over and over again. It's no wonder we feel like we're banging our head against a wall, because symbolically we are. It doesn't matter how many times we react with anger or tears or by shutting down, we don't get what we're truly after. And if peace of mind is what we are longing for, we only move further away. So what is it that keeps us doomed to repeat history? If we look at another layer underneath we can see that we have wacky thinking patterns in operation. It's our thoughts that lead us to have an emotional reaction and then a behavioral follow through. When we pause long enough to examine what we were thinking moments before our reaction we can see how unrealistic and illogical our thoughts tend to be. It is during frustrating and difficult times we tend to resort back to our childlike thinking, often riddled with extremes and polarities.

I remember a time when my dog, Jazzi, got into a box of decadent dark chocolates. As soon as I discovered it, I panicked. I had been warned about the poisonous effects dark chocolate can have on a dog. I started running around the house looking for my husband to save the day, but he had gone out. My mind went blank, my heart was racing and I couldn't think clearly enough to find the vet's phone number. I finally found it and called the number, but because it was Sunday it was closed and they left an emergency number to call. I called this and was told I needed to get our dog into the emergency vet as soon as possible. The only problem was that it was a couple of hours away from where we lived and the woman on the phone said our dog needed medical attention sooner than that. My panic froze and so did my body. Visions of my Jazzi dying were running through my mind.

Fortunately I realized what was happening; I was resorting back to an old pattern of catastrophizing which usually eliminated any chances of discovering a solution. I brought myself back into the present moment where I noticed Jazzi was not yet showing symptoms. I took a deep calming breath and told myself she would be okay, that I'd find a solution. I suddenly remembered a nearby neighbor was a retired veterinarian. A quick call to him led to a series of events which released Jazzi of her chocolate binge. I'm happy to say that Jazzi is still as spunky as ever and that I am much better at keeping the chocolate out of her reach.

When we can catch our thoughts in motion we can shift them in a new direction before it's too late. Eventually, with practice, we will create new neural pathways of a healthier mindset and won't have to watch our thoughts so closely. So what are your typical stress reactions and thought patterns?

Exercises on Identifying Reactions

Thoughts & Reactions

Below is a list of some common thought patterns and stress

reactions many of us resort to. Pick out your favorite habits and add any others that are not on the list.

* **Catastrophizing:** imagining that the situation will get worse and worse, and will affect everything around it. Continually repeating thoughts of disaster.

* **Panicking:** excessive worrying about what will happen to the point of feeling out of control. Similar to catastrophizing but with a faster pace leading to irrational behaviors.

* **All or Nothing Thinking:** everything is either all good or all bad, all right or all wrong and there is no in-between. If one thing goes wrong, suddenly the perspective is that everything is wrong.

* **Perfectionism:** things have to be done perfectly or they are no good and you feel like a failure. Often accompanies underlying judgmental thoughts that you are not good enough.

* **Beating Yourself Up:** constantly thinking negatively about yourself or finding fault with things you do. Follows perfectionism well.

* **Blaming Role:** blaming others for the situations you are in. Not taking responsibility for your part in creating your life circumstances. Thinking that others have more control over your life than you do.

* **Victim Role:** thinking that nothing you do will make a difference, things will not change and that you have no control over anything. Poor me attitude, hoping someone else will rescue you – goes well with the blaming role.

★ **Over-Responsibility:** taking on responsibility for others or taking on more of your fair share in a team effort. Thinking that you are the only one who can do it or do it well.

★ **Ostrich:** shutting down or hiding from what is happening. Thinking it will all go away if you focus on something else. A form of denial.

★ **Dramatizing:** over exaggerating a situation, thinking that your problem should be everyone's concern. Attention seeking behavior.

For each of your habitual stress reactions you identified from the list, brainstorm ideas about how you could respond in healthier ways. For example, if you tend to catastrophize, you could practice deep breathing to calm yourself, or use your thoughts to imagine all of the possible positive outcomes instead of the negative ones. If you fall into the role of the victim, you could repeat the affirmation that you are powerful and in control of your life, or you could remind yourself of all the wonderful things you have manifested in your life.

Stress Styles

It's fun to characterize our stress styles by giving them a name and humorous description. If we can laugh at ourselves and get a bit of separation from the traits we take on, we can loosen up their hold on us and begin to shift them. Have fun writing a colorful portrait of your unique stress style.

★ Pick up to three stress reactions you identified with from the list. Imagine that a character in a story has these traits and give this person a name that personifies these. Drawing from your own life experiences, but perhaps with some embellishment, write a brief description of how this character over reacts to stressful situations. Include the effects this reaction has on the character, those around them and the end results.

For example, here is my character description for my reactions of catastrophizing, panicking and being a perfectionist.

Princess Perfect (PP) discovers that she has missed a deadline for an important job. Her eyes bulge out, her breathing stops and her mind begins to race at 100 miles per minute. She envisions the end of her career, leading to bankruptcy and having to move home to her parents. She quickly calls everyone she knows asking for favors to help her get the job done right away. Her friends, obviously feeling pressured, quickly get new unlisted phone numbers. PP feels out of control and extremely small and helpless right now.

★ Now write a new scene in which the character responds to a similar situation with calm and ease. Describe what the character is thinking and how they are viewing the situation, how they feel and behave, and how this new way of thinking and responding affects them, others and the end result. Here is an example.

Ms Confident discovers her missed deadline and just as she is about to panic, she takes a deep breath, centers herself and reminds herself how this has happened before and it turned out okay. She laughs at herself for not paying closer attention to her day-timer and looks at it now to see where she can fit in time to work on this project. She contacts a colleague of hers to see if he is interested in taking on part of this work. She also contacts the person in charge of this project and explains the situation. The person in charge is very understanding and they create a new deadline. Ms Confident feels relaxed with a new sense of empowerment.

The next time you notice yourself slipping into the character that over reacts, see if you can stop, have a good laugh at yourself, and switch into the new character traits. What would you need to think and tell yourself to shift your reactions into calmness and ease?

Chapter 7

Shifting Your Reactions

Shifting into a new way of responding can take time. Our typical reactions are deeply ingrained so it will take awareness and practice to create new habitual responses. It's much like a stream or river; water takes the path of least resistance. If someone digs a trench in a new direction and blocks the path of the previous riverbed, the water flows in the new route and creates a deeper path over time. So it is with our habitual thinking and behaving; we need to stop our old patterns and create new pathways.

The first step to shifting into a new behavior is always awareness. When we catch ourselves thinking, feeling or reacting in our unhealthy ways, we can stop and choose a new perspective, attitude or behavior. We can remind ourselves that we are thinking unrealistic thoughts and feed ourselves more truthful, calming thoughts. We can look at the situation or person in a new way, from a different angle. We can choose to behave in a way that is different to our usual reactivity.

If I am beginning to panic and catastrophize because of an apparent problem, I can notice how I am reacting, take a deep breath and choose new thoughts. Instead of imagining the worst outcome, I can challenge myself to be more realistic or even imagine the best possible solution. If someone is being rude to me and I start to take it personally, I can expand my perspective by wondering if they've had a bad day or are going through a difficult time in their life. If the pressures are piling up in my life and my tendency is to distract myself or go into denial, I can notice my behaviors and instead do something completely different such as prioritizing my tasks and completing one at a time until they are done.

In order to make these shifts into newer, healthier and inspiring directions there are four very effective attitudes or ways of being we can apply that will support us in this transition. These are Acceptance, Ease, Amusement and Gratitude. Adopting these will lighten any situation, lift any mood, and transform any problem in a matter of seconds. I highly recommend you carry these with you and within you at all times.

Acceptance

Acceptance is the key to shifting chaos into calm, to making sense of things and bringing peace back into life. When I've facilitated corporate workshops on shifting stress and creating balance in life, there is often one person in the room who doesn't seem to need the workshop but is there to be with his or her co-workers. When I ask them what their secret is to not getting stressed out in life they each say the same thing: "I just accept things the way they are." Sounds simple enough, so why aren't most of us doing that? Is it because we associate accepting with condoning or with giving up or giving in? Are we afraid that if we accept the situation we're going to get stream rolled over by life? None of this is true of course. It's just that wacky mind of ours listening to the faint memories coded in our DNA of the dangers of accepting that lion with his fangs bared.

All acceptance is, is agreeing with reality, being with what is. It is saying to ourselves, "yes, this is happening", or "yes, this person is behaving this way". For those of us who need the illusion of being in control, we can look at it as allowing things to be what they are. Acceptance is more about not doing than taking any action; not denying, not judging, not resisting, not fighting, not running away. Just being with what is. We may not like it, but trying to resist what is, or deny it, or hide from it, only creates inner conflict, which in turn leads to outer turmoil. There is another way. There is a simpler, easier, softer way. It's the way of acceptance.

No matter what the situation, how irritating the person is, or how awful we feel, accepting it will bring us peace and calm. The main reason is because when we are not accepting something we are using energy to maintain an illusion or to hold up a wall between us and the situation or person, and this is tiring and frustrating. When we stop doing this we relax, find relief and detach from the situation or person long enough to see the bigger picture, the solution or the humor in it all.

To accept first requires a shift in perception. A shift from the perception that it is anything other than it is. Sometimes when we want people or situations to be different than they are we get stuck in the image of what we want instead of what is. We can expend huge amounts of energy wishing things were different than they are.

When we shift our perceptions we need to let go of judging the situation as bad or wrong. It is easy to get caught on the extremes of right or wrong, good or bad, all or nothing. The world seems to operate on these and many other dichotomies, yet they are very limiting as reality is much more encompassing than these extremes. We may not like things or people as they are, but to cast judgment upon them is what causes us pain, not the person or situation itself. By allowing the person to be just the way they are, or allowing the situation to be what it is in the moment, we expand our mind instead of constricting it. Instead of trying

47

to fit a square peg into a round hole we open up to additional possibilities. Possibilities which can not be seen when we are in denial or resistance. If we are searching for a pen but believe pens only come in blue casings, we will most likely miss the pens in red, green and other colored casings that could be sitting right before our eyes. It is the same with a difficult situation. If we are stuck on it being a certain way, a way that it currently is not, we will miss the richness of options that are available. Sometimes even apparent disasters, when embraced with open mindedness, can turn into the most amazing blessings. Who knew? No one knew at first, but by letting go of denial and resistance and moving into the flow of acceptance a space was opened, one flooded with possibilities.

Exercises for Practicing Acceptance

Try the following exercises as a way to become more accepting of yourself, others and situations in your life.

★ Imagine that someone who triggers or irritates you is standing in front of you, doing or saying their usual annoying behavior. Become aware of how you feel, what your thoughts are and what you feel like doing. Is your habit to shut down, try to change them, argue with them, or avoid them? What is the judgment you hold about them? Feel the emotion and energy behind the judgment. Where do you notice it in your body? Does it have a shape, color or texture? Imagine letting the judgment go. It might help to imagine it as something you are holding onto that you are putting down, or imagine the energy, color, or feeling of the judgment releasing out of your space. If you have any attachment to the judgment, or resistance to releasing it, let that go first and then the judgment. Now notice if you have any non-peaceful feelings about this person, and let them go as well. What is left underneath now? How do you feel about the person and their behavior now? Are you able to accept them or the situation more easily now?

★ Think of a problem in your life and notice how you feel about it and where in your body you carry these feelings. If you are not accepting the situation and feeling neutral or peaceful about it then notice what your thoughts and judgments are about it. Are you viewing the situation as right or wrong, good or bad? What would it be like to let these views go and accept the situation as it is? What other thoughts or judgments are you carrying? Are you judging or beating yourself up about it? Are you blaming someone else for it? Notice if you have any attachment to the thoughts and judgments or any resistance in letting them go. First let go of the attachment and resistance. Imagine it floating away from you as if it is an object. How does that feel? Now let go of the actual thoughts and judgments and notice what's underneath. Are there any uncomfortable feelings you need to acknowledge and accept before you can find peace? Let yourself process whatever emotions you need to as this will support you in moving into a place of acceptance.

★ The next time you encounter someone behaving in a way that irritates you, rather than going into resistance or trying to change them, see if you can simply accept them the way they are. See past their behavior to the person acting that way. What must they believe about themselves or life to be acting that way? What life experiences might they have had to program these behaviors? Who are they underneath?

★ The next time you don't like the situation you are experiencing but don't have an immediate solution, notice how you feel, what you are thinking and what your typical reactions are. If you are judging the situation, yourself or someone else as bad or wrong or hopeless or some other extreme, see if you can let any of the thoughts go. Notice how you feel releasing them. Notice if your perspective of the situation has shifted.

Ease

How do we stay in the flow of acceptance? By embracing a state of ease. The opposite of ease is effort and struggle. Whether we are struggling against external people or situations or our own internal thoughts and feelings, we are going against the flow of life. In the not so distant past, effort and struggle paid off, or so we were told. How many stories have we heard from our parents and grandparents about 'struggling through the depression times to have a better life' or 'the efforts and struggles of war to save our country' or how 'hard effort tilling the farm with your sweat and tears reaped a full harvest'. Work has been synonymous with effort and struggle and has been rewarded in many areas of our society. When we've put in long hard hours and overcome obstacles and challenges and have been stretched until we've nearly snapped, it somehow makes the accomplishment sweeter, doesn't it? We can hear all our co-workers, family and friends saying "way to go, you're such a hard worker, you're effort really paid off!" After several rounds of this we begin to wonder if it might be easier to embezzle all the funds from the company and take a permanent vacation, check into a nearby psychiatric ward for a wee break, or just go sit on the corner of a street and collect coins in a hat from now on. What we're really searching for is ease. But because we equate anything worthwhile with effort and struggle we sidestep ease. We don't realize that we can put our best into projects and do it with ease at the same time.

It's time we create a new equation. One where we see that struggle and effort leads to pain and frustration, and ease leads to flow and accomplishment. Just thinking about achieving something with ease can light up questions such as "will I deserve it then?" along with feelings of unworthiness and shame as if we stole the result. It also triggers fears that if we don't put in a hard effort or struggle to make it happen, then we might not be successful, we might fail. This is "past time" thinking, living out of an old paradigm. One that is based on beliefs that will slowly kill us from over worked nerves, high volumes of stress hormones, and suppressed immune systems. Putting time and energy into a project definitely pays off, but doing it from a state of ease and balance brings us to the goal quicker and with a healthier outcome overall.

We've all experienced the effects of effort and struggle: brains shutting down, ideas few and far between, and insights disappearing. And we've also had those moments of ease and relaxation where epiphanies abound. Effortless ease is the current way of life to achieve positive results. We know this deep inside our hearts, so how do we go about living life this way? By allowing things to unfold instead of trying to make them happen. By trusting that things work out. By listening to our inner knowing, our intuition. By breathing, relaxing and opening up to the abundance of opportunities that await us.

Exercises for Practicing Ease

Ease is a way of being; experiment and explore the following suggestions as a way to help you move into this state.

★ Get to know the difference between ease and effort through your body. Grip your hands into tight fists, clinch your jaw and tighten your whole body. Notice how you feel in this state and recognize this as a signal to shift into ease. Now breath, let go and relax. Notice how you feel when you are in a state of ease. Let this state move through your entire body. Try doing different activities from both of these states and notice how each affects your thoughts, mood and ability to perform the various activities. The more you become aware of what it feels like to be in effort, the sooner you will be able to shift into a state of ease.

★ Become aware of when you go into effort. Is it because of external demands, internal pressures, or wanting a certain outcome? Imagine what it would be like to let go of effort in one of these situations. Imagine dealing with things from a

51

state of ease, allowing things to unfold and taking action in a relaxed manner. Could you do this? What would happen? Will you try it next time?

★ Who do you often go into effort with? Is there any particular person who triggers this response in you? Imagine them standing in front of you, pushing your effort buttons. Now imagine shifting into a state of ease and responding from there. Try it for real the next time you encounter this person.

★ When you find yourself stuck in a frustrating situation, such as traffic, notice if you move into effort, as though gripping the wheel tighter and cursing under your breath will actually speed up the pace. It might quicken your heartbeat and blood pressure, but according to the laws of the Universe, it will probably slow traffic down, not speed it up. This is the theory that whatever we are experiencing internally is mirrored externally. So instead, try accepting the situation as it is, relax into it, use the time to practice deep breathing and then see if the traffic flow changes.

Amusement

When acceptance and ease seem to be too far to reach, then go for amusement. Laughter is the cure all for any malady and we don't have to go anywhere to get it; we have it right within ourselves. Studies have shown the many benefits of laughter on our mental, physical and emotional health. If laughter can boost our immune system then certainly it can shift our stress reactions. We can't be angry or anxious and amused at the same time, so it's our choice. Being amused raises our mood from dark to light, and it is in the lighter states that we feel at ease and become accepting. Now I'm not suggesting that the next time someone pushes your buttons, to point a finger at them and laugh at the size of their nose, or belt out "ha, ha, you deal with it". I'm also not talking about harsh forms of sarcasm or belittling humor. I'm referring to the state of amusement. It has a vibration, like all emotions. It's a light, bubbly state, as if all of our cells are giggling like small children. Being in this mood helps us to see the lighter side of things. It moves us out of resistance and helps us to put life into perspective instead of creating drama out of minor mishaps. Even dealing with major problems becomes easier when we can laugh at ourselves and the bizarre situations we find ourselves in.

Exercises for Practicing Amusement

We could all use more fun and laughter in our lives. Try these tips to see if you can tickle your funny bone.

★ Become aware of how often you laugh. Do you keep your amusement hidden? Could you let it out a bit more? Are you able to see the lighter side of life or do you look for the problems? Set your intention to find the humor in things, even if it means laughing at how serious you take things.

★ Focus on doing something fun or funny each day. It could be anything from reading the comics in the morning and sharing them with co-workers to watching a comedy to taking part in a zany adventure. Brainstorm a list of all the fun and funny things you can think of and then pick one or more to do each day.

★ Think of something funny that makes you laugh. Feel the energy of laughter in your body. Let this vibration flow throughout every cell and the spaces between the cells. Imagine turning up the volume of amusement within you. Notice how this feels and how it affects your thoughts and emotions. Allow yourself to be in this state as much as possible so it becomes a normal way of being. Even when you are dealing with serious issues, you can still blanket them with a state of amusement so they flow more easily.

The next time you are feeling stressed, just imagine turning up your amusement dial and let the energy flow through your body.

★ When you are busy working or trying to accomplish something important notice how serious you are. Can you focus on your work, be responsible and productive, as well as be light and amused at the same time? Try it and find out.

Gratitude

When we can be thankful for all that life brings us we have reached enlightenment. Well, maybe not, but we have stepped even higher than acceptance, gone deeper than ease, and become lighter than amusement. The state of gratitude vibrates at a very high frequency. It feels even brighter than joy. Cultivating gratitude into our daily lives allows us to rise above petty nuisances, to surpass the depths of despair, and to see serendipity working in our favor at all times. It's what keeps us focused on the benefits instead of the problems.

It's easy to find what's not working in our lives, in our society, in our world. It takes another shift in perception to see what is working. As the saying goes, 'misery loves company' and people do enjoy congregating to share their mishaps and misfortunes. It's almost as if getting together to share success stories would be sacrilege. Perhaps we're concerned that shining a light on our happiness might reflect the gloom in someone else's life. Or we're afraid that we're the only one with something positive in our lives and if others find out, no one will like us. If we act like "nothin's no good no how", then we won't disturb the equilibrium amongst our co-workers and friends. Yet griping about what we don't like, what we don't have, and who's getting on our nerves only creates a negative spiral. We get into competition about who's had a worse day, a worse year, a worse life. And it doesn't stop there because as soon as we start to talk about someone else (behind their back of course) we pump up the volume and we all contribute our opinions on what an irritating knob the person is. My Mom used to say that whatever criticisms we had about others, we secretly held about ourselves. Ouch, that hurts, but it's true. Time to go back to step one - Acceptance.

How can we focus on what's good in our life? By doing just that. Instead of dwelling on upsetting events in the paper or on the news, we can read or listen to something inspiring. Instead of talking to someone who brings us down with their complaints, we can contact someone who makes us laugh. Instead of looking for problems we can look for solutions. Rather than beating ourselves up, we can choose to be kind to ourselves. We can brainstorm all of the possible positive outcomes to our situation or we can imagine all of the worst scenarios. We always have a choice, and as we know, what we focus on grows so do we want to feed our pessimism or our optimism?

When we reflect on the wonderful things in our lives, we feel good, it's that simple. And if we shine a light on the good things during the bad times, we open up to hope; the place where new possibilities lay.

Exercises for Practicing Gratitude

Gratitude is a wonderful state to be in on an ongoing basis. It connects you to the Source of all life and to the abundance life has to offer you. Use the following tools as a way to maintain the grace of gratitude in your life.

★ Make a list of all the things you are currently grateful for in your life (try to fill the whole page) and put it somewhere you can easily see it. Read your gratitude list daily and at any times you are feeling down, frustrated or cranky.

★ Just for fun, get together with a friend and spend 5 minutes griping about all the things you are not happy about in your life. Then notice how you feel physically, emotionally and mentally. Then spend 5 minutes sharing all of the things you are grateful for, and notice how you feel.

★ It would be great if we could install a measuring scale inside our heads to keep track of our attitudes. It could let off a loud warning beep when we're going down the slippery slope of negativity and we could shift our focus to something more positive. It's only through our self-awareness that we can know what direction our thoughts and words are trailing off into. Try becoming more aware of your thought patterns. When you notice you are being negative or critical, gently shift your attention to something you are grateful for.

★ Before you go to sleep at night, go over your day and be thankful for all the gifts, lessons, growth and other positive aspects you are aware of. Then release it all with the intention of creating another positive day tomorrow.

★ Notice if there is anything or anyone in your life that you are not grateful for. If you are feeling judgmental or resentful, this may indicate a need for forgiveness. Is there someone you need to forgive, including yourself? Forgiveness doesn't mean condoning; it is a gift you give yourself. Forgiveness allows the release of judgments, negative attitudes and pain that has been taking up space in your body and energy system. By forgiving we are letting go, releasing and freeing ourselves. Forgiveness begins with acceptance and ends with love.

You can take acceptance, ease, amusement and gratitude one step further by adding the energy of love. The next time you are faced with a difficult situation or person, feel the love that is inside of you. The essence of love is at our core, but if you are having difficulty connecting with it think of someone or something you love to help generate the feeling. Then let that energy of love flow throughout your whole body, down to all the cells and the spaces in between. Now look at the person or situation through the eyes of love. It's difficult to respond in any stressful way when we are bubbling forth with love.

Chapter 8

Uncovering Your Motives & Payoffs

What happens when we bring all of the acceptance, ease, amusement and gratitude we can summon to our life situations only to fall back into the same old stress reactions? Then it's time to look at the incentives for our behaviors. There's a reason we've been reacting in these ways. We are intelligent, logical human beings who know how to perform all sorts of manipulations in order to get our needs met. So what needs are we trying to meet anyway? Underneath any behavior is a motive, and following that is a payoff. All we have to do is play detective and investigate our lives a little further.

I was raised to be a good worrier. It was a simple mistake; my chaotic family environment was created to raise a good warrior but I misplaced a couple of vowels and ended up a full fledged worrier. Nevertheless it all worked out in the end as I finally got my warrior training and I now understand the difference between the two. People who worry tend to be filled with fear and are either too immobilized by it to take any action or are so wound up they take unnecessary action. I was the wound up one. Warriors on the other hand are cool, calm and collected and know when to strike and when to sit back and wait patiently. They have strong boundaries and don't get taken advantage of. It's taken me quite a few years to develop my inner warrior. I had to learn to think differently, view situations in a new light, and trust that things would work out without me resorting to old tactics.

Before I could completely convert my worrier tendencies into a warrior stance, I needed to look at what was hooking me into worrying, catastrophizing and panicking. I knew deep inside that this wasn't my true nature, no matter how comfortable it felt, and that continuing on with it wasn't serving me in discovering my intrinsic self. This was enough reason for me to dig deeper into my patterns.

When we discover what drives us to do the things we do and what the ensuing rewards are, we create huge leverage for change. We see how insidious these motives and payoffs are and we can't help but loosen their hold on us because we are disturbed by their impact on our lives. I discovered that one of the motives for my worrying was the false belief that I was responsible for other people's lives. It didn't matter who they were, as long as they were involved in my life in someway, I was somehow responsible for them. The reward I received for spending countless hours in a state of frenzy over someone else's drama was the illusion that this behavior could somehow affect the outcome. Fixating on other's problems gave me a false sense of hope to hang on to until things worked themselves out and I could finally relax. The wishful thinking part of me would say that if I hadn't worried, things might have turned out worse, and of course, it would somehow be my fault. This was all unconscious thinking and belief systems buried deep within me from when I was a child and trying to cope with the chaos in my family. Back then having false illusions might have somehow helped me to make it into adulthood relatively unscathed. As an adult all it did was help me to attract people into my life who fit my old patterns, like two pieces of a puzzle fitting perfectly together.

Awareness of our motives and payoffs is crucial to unblocking the barriers to our health and happiness.

Exercises for Uncovering the Motives & Payoffs

Completing the Sentence

One of the best ways to find out what motivates us to do what we do is to let our unconscious mind roam. Through these ramblings we can find a few nuggets of truth that will help us to consciously move in a new direction. Try the following sentence completion exercises and see what insights you discover.

★ Take a piece of paper and at the top write down one of your stress reaction styles (such as 'catastrophizing') and then write: helps me to . . . and write down as many answers that come to mind, listing them down the page. Don't try to find answers, just write down anything that pops up no matter how silly it seems. Once you get rolling, you're unconscious will spit out the truth. When you've exhausted your list, go over it and circle the statements that jump out at you.

★ On another sheet of paper write at the top: I need to (your stress reaction style such as 'panic') because . . . and list all of the things that come to mind. Or try 'If I don't (your reaction style such as 'worry')" . . . and list what comes up. Circle any important statements.

★ Explore the circled items from each of the sentence completion exercises to see what insights come to you. If you feel puzzled or stuck with any of the answers you came up with, try doing a sentence completion with them. Can you see what your motives and payoffs are for your stress reaction styles? Over the next few days set your intention to become even more aware of the underlying motives and payoffs, and watch as new insights surface.

Chapter 9

Exposing the Consequences & Costs

Sometimes being aware of the motives and payoffs for our stress reactions is enough to inspire us to create new responses. But sometimes we need to propel ourselves further by looking at the consequences of our stress reactions and the associated costs. If we can see how our blaming behavior keeps us in a perpetual state of anger, which raises our blood pressure, we might be willing to trade it in for something more calming. Or if we realize that a perspective of victim-hood causes us to give up our power, which deepens our state of hopelessness, and leads us to isolate we may prefer to take on a brighter outlook rather than sink further into a black hole.

Once I discovered how I was hooked in to being over-responsible, worrying and catastrophizing, all I needed to push me over the edge to clarity was to see the consequences and painful costs associated with these behaviors. The equation was simple then. Getting others approval, strokes and feeling needed = feeding my insecurities, being taken advantage of and exhausting my nervous system. Versus, validating myself and my skills, letting others be responsible for themselves, and focusing more on me than others = feeling good about myself, having more time and energy to be creative and productive, and being healthy overall. It wasn't a tough decision to make. It just required finding new ways of thinking, feeling and reacting.

Exercises for Exposing the Consequences & Costs

Mapping the Consequences & Costs

Here is a creative mind mapping technique to try which will help you to see all of the consequences and costs associated with your stress reaction style. Take a blank sheet of paper and follow these steps.

★ Draw a circle in the center of the page and write the name of your typical stress reaction in it (i.e. 'Drama Queen'). Draw lines as spokes coming out from this circle to five other circles (leaving enough room for additional spokes from these).

★ Label these outer five circles: emotional, physical, mental, spiritual and behavioral. Insides each of these five circles write the consequences you experience as a result of your stress reaction style. So for example, in the mental circle, you might list: racing thoughts, negative thinking and mental exhaustion. In the physical circle you might list: knot in stomach, headache and tired. Fill in each of the circles until they feel complete.

★ From these five circles use lines to branch off and list all of the additional costs you experience from these consequences. Branching off of the mental circle you might end up with: can't concentrate on work, don't finish work on time, end up working on weekend and disappoint kids. And from the physical circle you might have: need to take pain medication, too tired to exercise after work, nap all weekend and don't do creative projects.

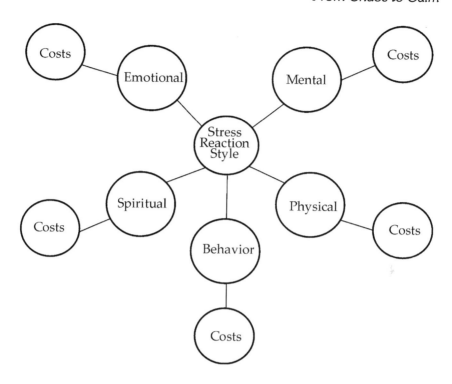

★ Now go through the same mind mapping exercise but in the center circle write down a response style you would like to have, such as centered and calm, or clear and proactive. Then in the five outer circles, write down the positive emotional, physical, mental, spiritual and behavioral effects you would experience as a result of this response. Finally, write down all the positive effects that would stem from these five circles into the rest of your life. You can use these as motivators, goals and reminders of how you want to be and what you want to create in your life.

Chapter 10

Satisfying Your Underlying Needs

Going over what motives us to react the way we do and acknowledging the hidden payoffs, no matter how twisted they seem, is a great catalyst for change. Adding the consequences and costs to the pile, the discomfort of it all becomes so unbearable we're on our knees begging for answers. We humans tend to need a certain amount of pain and discomfort before we are willing to let go of the old comfy ways and embark on new territory. Practicing acceptance, ease, amusement and gratitude can support us in shifting into new perspectives. But to create long term change, we need to satisfy the parts of us that are longing for approval, attention, safety or whatever motivated us into our initial reactions and behaviors in the first place.

We all have certain ways of trying to meet our needs and when those ways are no longer effective, it is time to try something new, even if it feels unfamiliar or uncomfortable at first. The new way may not satisfy the need right away, but over time it will have a lasting impact. Habits don't form overnight so it's important to give ourselves the time and space to practice, assimilate and integrate new, healthier ways of being in the world if we want to create positive change in our lives.

Exercises for Satisfying Underlying Needs

Brainstorming Solutions

Write down your top 5 needs from the Needs Assessment in chapter 1, as well as the Motives and Payoffs that you identified in chapter 8. With each of these, brainstorm a list of how many ways you can satisfy your needs, motives and payoffs in a healthier, more balanced manner. Let yourself come up with zany ideas as well as practical ones and then decide which ones you will implement.

For example, if feeling safe was a motivator for one of your stress reactions, you might create a list that includes:

- repeat mantra "I am safe" whenever I get triggered
- scream at the top of my lungs "I am safe"
- breathe deeply for 5 minutes
- focus on something more positive
- drop what I'm doing and go see a funny movie
- break down the "To Do" list into manageable parts
- phone a friend for comfort
- do yoga and meditation regularly

Or if feeling important was a payoff for a stress reaction style you might have:

- repeat affirmation that "I am enough just being me"
- tell people my time is too valuable to take on petty tasks
- find ways to release feelings of inadequacy
- find ways to build self-esteem and self-confidence

You might then need to brainstorm further ideas on how to

release feelings or build new inner states. These might involve visualization exercises, counseling, coaching, empowering books, CD's, or workshops and so on. There's nothing more important than giving yourself what you truly need.

Intuiting Solutions

Close your eyes, take a few deep breaths, be grounded and centered, and from this calm still place ask yourself what it is you need right now to fulfill your specific needs. Let your imagination show you, tell you or bring you into the experience of it. Reflect on ways you can meet these needs on a regular basis.

Chapter 11

Seeing the Bigger Picture

Our stress triggers, reactions, motives, payoffs and consequences all fit into the bigger picture of our life. When we can stand back and look over the years to see how this pattern has unfolded, we can see how it has served us and where we have become stuck or off purpose. It is then easier to know what step we need to take in order to move in the direction we want to go. We can look at the overall picture of our life or we can break it down and look at our patterns with money, relationships, career and so on.

One place to start is with the situations and circumstances that trigger our stress reactions. Work is one that most of us can relate to, yet each person's pattern may be unique. One person's pattern may be that they are coasting along fine with a comfortable amount of work, which is interesting and enjoyable. Then before they know it their workload has piled up so high they have to put their in-basket on the floor in order to reach the top of the pile. They start to feel pressured, overwhelmed, and they start skipping lunch in order to get ahead on their work. They are not enjoying their work anymore, yet are spending more time doing it; a five-day work week has turned into a six-day week. Eventually they get sick and have to miss a few days of work. Someday this gets resolved, whether they manage to catch up on their own, or office support is brought in to help out, or they take a sick leave and someone else catches up for them. Things are running smooth again until one day the cycle starts over all over.

Another's pattern may be that they have difficulty finding work that not only stimulates them but that pays them the value of their skills. So they settle for a less interesting job with low pay in hopes that they will be promoted in a year or so. Time goes on and they find they are either being shuffled around from one boring task to another, or they take on more responsible work but are not compensated for it. Their supervisor may keep telling them that a better position will open up soon for them, or may give endless excuses for why the company can't pay them more for the wonderful work they do. After a few years of this they finally quit, feeling angry and abused. Over time they let go of this, find a new job and the pattern continues because they haven't healed the underlying issues of self-esteem or self-worth.

If we are behaving a certain way in one area of our life, chances are we are repeating this in other areas of our life. It's easier to see what is going on when we look at someone else's pattern. The person with work over-load, most likely has a stress reaction trait of over-responsibility, perhaps with some catastrophizing thrown in. Their underlying motive may be that in order to feel good enough they need to take on more than their share and they don't feel they deserve to set boundaries. The payoff is that they get stroked for being such a hard worker, and perhaps even pitied and cared for when they get sick. The consequences are not pleasant, yet not enough to deter the ongoing cycle.

The under valued and under paid employee on the other hand probably has a victim stress reaction trait, perhaps with a blaming or ostrich one thrown in. Their underlying motive may be a bit trickier to perceive; perhaps it reinforces their belief that they are not worthy so they get to stay being a victim. The payoff could be even more obscure, such as an attachment to anger or feeling small, but the consequences are obvious; a lack of fulfillment in work and lack of financial abundance.

So this is the dark side of our patterns. What about the brighter side? It can't all be about self-sabotaging can it? I don't think so. When we actually write down or draw on a chart our patterns, at first we will see the obvious destructive habits. We can make note of the motives and payoffs and start to look at our underlying beliefs. Then we can look at how these situations and behaviors have triggered our growth and evolution. We can see how the times of struggle taught us to fend for ourselves, or being walked over one too many times led to developing strong clear boundaries, or searching for external strokes led us to discovering our inner self-worth. Many of the experiences we have lead to lessons and gifts, which are needed later on in life for specific purposes. Viewing our patterns can guide us to these lessons sooner. We can learn the hard slow way by playing them out to the bitter end, or we can take a closer look now, learn what we need to and change course with ease and empowerment.

Exercises on the Big Picture

Drawing the Pattern

To see the bigger picture of your life, choose a pattern that you are aware of repeating that causes you to feel stressed. It may be related to work, finances, relationships, health or a blend of one or more. Take a blank piece of paper and follow these steps.

★ Draw a picture or chart to represent the ups and downs of this pattern repeating itself over time. It may look like a roller coaster in the example below, an upward spiral, or a symbol that has meaning for you.

★ Note on your chart/picture what events and experiences are happening along the way. Then note any reactions, motives, payoffs or consequences you are aware of.

★ Write down the lessons you have learned as a result of this pattern.

★ Write down the gifts you've received as a result of this pattern.

★ Write down the current lessons you need to learn in order to shift your pattern in the direction you want it take.

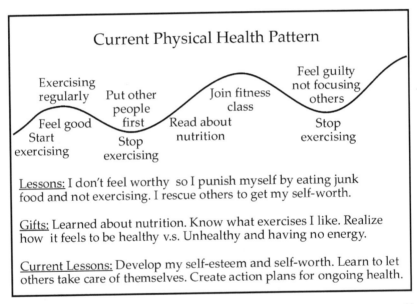

Current Physical Health Pattern

Exercising regularly   Put other people first   Join fitness class   Feel guilty not focusing others

Feel good   Read about nutrition   Stop exercising
Start exercising   Stop exercising

Lessons: I don't feel worthy so I punish myself by eating junk food and not exercising. I rescue others to get my self-worth.

Gifts: Learned about nutrition. Know what exercises I like. Realize how it feels to be healthy v.s. Unhealthy and having no energy.

Current Lessons: Develop my self-esteem and self-worth. Learn to let others take care of themselves. Create action plans for ongoing health.

You can go as deep as you like with the thoughts, motives, payoffs, costs and consequences to your stress pattern. The more aware you are of your patterns, the easier they will be to change.

Creating a New Pattern

Take out another blank piece of paper and draw a new pattern representing how you would like to live your life in this area with the reactions, motives, payoffs, and consequences you would like to experience.

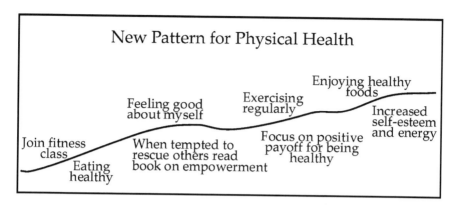

Regarding the new pattern you want to create, ask yourself the following questions and write down whatever comes to mind.

★ What would help motivate me to create this healthier pattern?

★ What would I have to let go of in order to create this new pattern?

★ What would I have to embrace?

★ What would I have to do differently?

★ What am I willing to do this week to move in this direction?

Beliefs

"Human beings, by changing the inner beliefs of their minds, can change the outer aspects of their lives."
William James

Beliefs are the foundation upon which we build our life structure. If our beliefs are solid, supportive and based in truth we will most likely create a life filled with trust and abundance. If on the other hand our beliefs are flimsy, limiting and based on falsehoods, we may very easily manifest a life filled with fear and scarcity.

Our beliefs are deeply rooted within us, so much so that we don't always know what they are. Yet we base our thoughts, emotions and reactions on them. There is a whole world of possibilities out there, but we filter our perceptions through our beliefs in order to make sense of the world. The shade of lenses we are wearing or the size of blinders we have on will determine what we see and how we interpret it. This is why two people can have a totally different understanding of the same situation. It's no wonder so much conflict ensues around the world.

Because our life patterns stem from our beliefs we can change our direction by changing our beliefs. We may want more money, but if we carry an underlying belief in scarcity we either won't earn it or we'll find all sorts of ways to spend it so we end up broke again. It doesn't matter how much income we have as somehow the bills will get more expensive, things will break down and an apparent stream of bad luck will occur to suck all our financial resources away from us. This has been a financial pattern for many, but when we look at the bigger picture by charting it and noting the motives and payoffs, we start to see the underlying beliefs in operation. When we put together a few pieces of our history puzzle we see how grandpa's life of struggle led to our father's belief in scarcity and money hoarding behaviors which affected our beliefs around finances and the lack of. It's the same with any pattern we have in our life. Somewhere along the line we picked up messages from our family, school, and society about the game called life. Our own experiences further cemented these rules into our psyche and voila; we have an unconscious formula to follow in creating our lives.

Often when we don't have what we say we want in our lives, there is a limiting belief sabotaging our perspectives and behaviors. If we say we want a committed relationship yet have not found the 'right' partner or have not been able to sustain a relationship for very long, then chances are deep down we have a belief that is in conflict with our desire. Perhaps we believe we are not worthy and will be rejected or abandoned and won't be able to tolerate the pain, so we prevent ourselves from having this experience by not seeing available partners or we reinforce the belief by choosing unsuitable partners. If our lives are running smoothly and enjoyably then we don't need to dig any further, but if our lives are crumbling and tumbling around us, its time to dig out the rubble and build a new foundation.

Chapter 12

Investigating Your Beliefs

What would a person's life be like if they believed there is more than enough time, money and love to go around? What if they believed they were capable of doing anything they wanted in their life? What if they believed they were totally safe and could trust their instincts about others completely? What if they believed they deserve to do the work they love, and live a life full of ease and joy? How rewarding and enjoyable would their life be?

What would a person's life be like if they believed there's never enough time, money or love? What if they believed they were not competent or capable or good enough to do what they really want in their life? What if they believed the world is a scary place to live and that they can't trust others? What if they believed they had to work hard and struggle in order to live a decent life? How rewarding and enjoyable would their life be?

What is your life like? If your life is full of over-busyness, struggle or chaos then you must carry beliefs that support this. If you want your life to be peaceful, calm and balanced then you need to adopt beliefs that support this.

Exercises on Discovering Your Beliefs

People's Beliefs

When we tune into our beliefs about other people in general we discover that this often reflects our own beliefs about ourselves and life. Write down your first responses to the following questions.

★ People with lots of money...

★ People with lots of time...

★ People who work hard...

★ People who put others first...

★ People who put themselves first...

★ People who have an easy life...

There is no right or wrong answers here. Only indications of how you view the world and how this leads to what you create in your life.

Character Beliefs

Just as perceiving someone else's motives and payoffs for their stress reactions is easier than seeing our own at first glance, guessing another's core beliefs is simpler than observing our own. Sometimes it helps to step back and imagine a different character living our life and ask them questions about their beliefs. Create a fictional character and imagine that they are living your life with your circumstances and situations. For each set of unhealthy circumstances or situations, brainstorm a list of beliefs that this character might have in the following areas.

★ What might they believe about the world? That it's not safe, fair or just etc.?

★ What might they believe about other people? That they are judgmental, critical, uninterested etc.?

★ What might they believe about themselves? That they can't take good care of themselves, that they are not good enough, not worthy etc.?

Go over the possible beliefs you came up with and notice which ones are true for you.

Family Beliefs

Explore beliefs you may have picked up from your family about money, relationships, work, fun, recreation, and any other aspects of life. Reflect on each family member's beliefs to see which ones you have operating in your life.

Intuiting Your Beliefs

To discover your beliefs around having balance in your life, close your eyes, be grounded and centered, and finish the following sentences.

★ When I am responding to life with my typical stress reactions, I believe…

★ When I am responding to life with acceptance, ease, amusement and gratitude, I believe…

Open your eyes and write down your responses.

Chapter 13

Changing Your Beliefs

When we have a belief that creates a block or resistance to having something we really want in our life, it can masquerade as busyness, procrastination or boredom. When we want to reduce stress and create more balance in our life but keep telling ourselves, and anyone else who'll listen, "I'm too busy to learn about stress" or "I'll do it as soon as find some time", we know that underneath lies a distorted belief. This belief re-routes our truth into wacky thought patterns, feelings and behaviors. Once we can root out the limiting belief, we will discover our truth or at least a blank slate where we can write a new supportive belief. Much like the thoughts we choose to think, we can select our beliefs as well. From there we will think and feel differently, take new actions and reach a new destiny. It only takes a slight change of direction to create a completely different outcome.

Exercise on Changing Your Beliefs

Releasing the Old & Creating the New

Changing beliefs involves identifying limiting beliefs, letting them go and creating truthful and supportive ones. Here is a step-by-step exercise to take you through this process.

★ Take a piece of paper and at the top label it: Limiting Beliefs. On the left hand side of the paper, write down all of the situations, behaviors and stress reaction patterns you are not happy with. On the right hand side of the paper, write down the underlying beliefs that correspond with each of these. Write down any additional limiting beliefs that come to mind.

Limiting Beliefs	
Situations/Reactions/Behaviors	Underlying Beliefs
Over busy, too many things to do	Not enough time
I have too many tasks to do	No support, I have to do it all
Perfectionism- have to do it perfect the first time – if it's not done right, why bother.	If its not done right I am a failure – people will judge me and reject me if I'm not perfect
Feel guilty when not busy, then feel antsy or anxious	I'm not worthy – have to prove my worth – I don't deserve to relax

★ Hold the Limiting Beliefs piece of paper in your hand and walk around the room, imagine that each step you take is a step into your future with these beliefs. Notice how you feel physically, emotionally, mentally, and spiritually holding these beliefs. What do you think your life will be like 5 years in the future with these beliefs? How about 10 years in the future?

★ Let go of these beliefs for now by putting them down on the table. Take another piece of paper and at the top label it: Supportive Beliefs. On the left hand side, write down all of the things going well in your life. On the right hand side of the paper write down the underlying supportive beliefs that correspond with these situations. Write down any other supportive beliefs you have.

Supportive Beliefs

Situations/Responses/Behaviors	Underlying Beliefs
I'm a good parent and friend	*I am kind and loving*
I'm patient with my children	*I am patient and supportive*
I organize and plan well	*I am intelligent and visionary*
I come up with great ideas	*I am creative*

★ Look back over your Limiting Belief sheet. With each limiting belief, draw a line through it to cross it out and think of a new supportive belief to replace this with and write it down on your Supportive Beliefs sheet.

Supportive Beliefs	
Situations/Responses/Behaviors	Underlying Beliefs
I'm a good parent and friend	I am kind and loving
I'm patient with my children	I am patient and supportive
I organize and plan well	I am intelligent and visionary
I come up with great ideas	I am creative
	There's plenty of time
	I can receive support from others
	I can learn from mistakes
	People like me for who I am
	I am worthwhile just being me
	Relaxing is good for my health

★ Take your Supportive Beliefs sheet and hold it in your hand while you walk around the room. Imagine that each step you take is a step into your future with these more positive beliefs. Notice how you feel physically, emotionally, mentally, and spiritually holding these beliefs. What do you think your life will be like 5 years in the future with these beliefs? How about 10 years in the future?

★ If you are ready to completely let go of your Limiting Beliefs then crumple or tear the sheet up and throw it in the garbage or burn it in a fire while setting your intention to let all of these beliefs go.

★ Keep your Supportive Beliefs near you so you can read them daily to reinforce them into your mind and heart. If any negative thoughts or feelings arise as you do this, imagine releasing these out of your space. Then counter them with realistic, truthful statements and feel the positive energy from doing this.

Whenever you are aware of a thought or an underlying belief, ask yourself if it empowers or disempowers you. From this place you can choose to let it go or reinforce it.

Life

"At the heart of it, mastery is practice. Mastery is staying on the path."

George Leonard

Creating ongoing balance in life requires ongoing awareness, daily attitude shifts and new ways of behaving. Once we realize that we are the ones in control of our balance, and always have been, and we stop beating ourselves up for the chaos we've brought into our lives, we can settle into a new way of life. We set our intention for our unique state of balance, we catch ourselves when we are careening away from it, we use whatever tools we have to bring peace into our lives, we weed out limiting beliefs and adopt supportive ones, and we carry on as usual. It's that simple. It may not seem that simple at first. It's like learning to drive a stick shift. At first we may feel frustrated and awkward, jerking along the road, but eventually everything falls into place and we wonder what all the fuss was about. We still need to keep our eyes on the road and our hands on the wheel to make sure we are going in the direction we want to go, but it becomes an effortless task. It's the same with creating balance in our life. We bring our awareness to what we are thinking, feeling and doing, and we make whatever adjustments we need in order to stay on course. After a while, we're just living this wonderful, blissful life and we look back on the old life as if it were someone else's. And it was in a way. It was us covered up with beliefs, programming and reactions that didn't reflect who we really were. When we let go of what's not us, the real us emerges with clarity and a renewed sense of enthusiasm and zest for living. We discover our true desires and purpose in life and nothing can hold us back – look out world, here we come!

Chapter 14

Creating Ongoing Balance

When we've honestly looked at our lives, owned our stress reactions, identified the motives and payoffs, and unearthed the limiting beliefs fueling them, change happens naturally. Awareness is the biggest factor in shifting patterns. Why would any of us want to continue doing something we now know is unhealthy, unproductive and basically destructive to our lives? Masochism perhaps, addiction likely, unconsciousness for sure. It's easy to go unconscious and let the old patterns slip back into their comfortable groove. And before you know it, chaos is ruling once again. To keep the balance flowing, we need to heighten our awareness and actively practice new healthy behaviors until they have been rooted in place. This may take time, but aren't we worth it?

Exercises for Creating Ongoing Balance

Here are some tools you can practice daily to keep balance in the forefront. Some of them are a recap on previous exercises and some are new. You might want to try one or two each day until you integrate them and then move on to others, or you might want to customize your own package of tools to use regularly.

Reflecting Back

An exercise that is helpful to do in order to bring your life back into perspective is to imagine you are on your deathbed, reflecting over your life. What would you have wanted to spend more time doing? And what would you have preferred to spend less time doing?

One Piece at a Time

Choose one area of your life that you would like to have more balanced (look over your balance assessments to get an idea of where you most need to pay attention or close your eyes and reflect on this intuitively). It might be an internal aspect such as your thought patterns or emotional reactions, or it might be an external aspect such as your workload or social life. Come up with one or two ways to enhance this part of your life and bring it more into balance. Focus on it for one week and next week move onto another area of your life.

Ideal Balance

Imagine your ideal state of balance using all of your senses. Spend 5 minutes at the beginning each day or on a break envisioning this and set your intention to create this in your life. Intention is powerful as it connects all of your own internal resources with all of the world's external resources to bring your vision to reality.

Expressing Your Ideal Balance

Once you have imagined your ideal balance, use crayons, felt pens or paint to express the energy of this vision onto paper. Let whatever colors, shapes and images be drawn without thinking about it. Or create a collage to represent this vision using magazine clippings, colored paper, pressed flowers and so on. Just looking at this visual expression of your ideal balance will inspire you to manifest it throughout your day.

Affirm Balance

Use affirmations to support your ability to create balance in your life. You might write and repeat to yourself something like "I am continually creating balance in my life", or "my life is calm and peaceful", or if there is an underlying belief that triggers stressful reactions you can create an affirmation that dispels it such as "I am safe in this moment and all my needs are taken care of". The important part of affirmations is that they be in the present tense, be stated in the positive, and reflect your inner truth beyond the limiting beliefs.

In order to counteract any doubts or negative thoughts about your affirmation, write down your affirmation repeatedly on a sheet of paper. Notice the countering thoughts and imagine releasing them as you write down your affirmation each time. Keep writing until the affirmation feels good and doesn't have a negative charge. Post your affirmation in places you will see throughout the day.

Honoring Needs & Values

Check in with yourself regularly to see if you are honoring your needs and values instead of your fears and scarcity thoughts. By staying true to what uplifts you and sparks your passion you will naturally find balance in life. When making important decisions ask yourself which choice will honor your needs and values the most. Then ask yourself if this choice will bring you closer to balance or move you further away.

From Chaos to Calm

If at any time you feel you are lost in chaos and you don't know where to begin, close your eyes and ask yourself the following questions and then write down the answers:

★ What do I need to say no to?

★ What do I need to say yes to?

★ What do I need to let go of?

★ What do I need to embrace?

Focus on Acceptance, Ease, Amusement & Gratitude

What you focus on grows, so practice bringing acceptance, ease, amusement and gratitude into your life on a regular basis. You might want to focus on one a day and keep rotating them or find ways to blend them together. Notice which of them are easier for you and which are more difficult. For the ones that are more difficult, spend 5 minutes a day imagining being in this state and let the energy of it flow throughout your whole body, melting away any blocks.

Be in the Here & Now

When we are fully in the present moment, we automatically feel more balanced. It is when part of us in stuck in the past or rehearsing the future that we feel overwhelmed. It's like watching a snowstorm. When you try to see where the flakes are coming from or watch them fall all at once they just whiz by your sight. Yet when you let your eyes follow them at their present pace they seem to slow down.

Tools for being in the present moment include:

★ *Breathing*: focusing on your breath will slow down your mind, bring stillness and increase your energy circulation, all of which support you in being here and now.

★ *Centering*: being in the center of your head where you connect with your neutrality, truth and the 'you' who is bigger than all the 'stuff' going on in your life.

★ *Grounding*: being grounded in your body helps you to be in the present moment, to breathe easier and to release tension from your body.

★ *Noticing*: seeing what is happening around you in the moment or becoming aware of what you are currently feeling inside of you will bring you back into the present. Noticing your feelings and staying with them, even the uncomfortable ones, will allow them to release with ease.

★ *Creativity*: doing a spontaneous creative activity will bring you out of your past or future thoughts and into the flow of now.

Solution Focused

If you find your mind getting stuck on analyzing your stress or trying to figure out the causes, give yourself a break by instead focusing on solutions. Ask yourself questions such as "how many ways can I find to bring ease into my life?" or "what other possible solutions are there to this", or "how can I see the humor in this?" or "I wonder how many times I can be in the present moment today?" As you go through your day, your mind will be working in the background to bring you the solutions.

Collecting Your Energy

When you are feeling scattered or depleted it may be time to bring your energy back into your own space. As we go through the day we put a lot of our attention on work, projects, and others. Wherever our focus goes, our energy follows. To bring your energy back into your space, focus inwardly and imagine calling all of your energy back from the people and projects you have been focusing on while releasing their energy back to them.

Meditation

Meditating on a regular basis will help you to create an internal balance, which will then expand outwardly into your life. There are many forms of meditation, but one simple one is to sit comfortably with arms and legs uncrossed and close your eyes. Be grounded in your body with the focus in the center of your head. To calm your thoughts begin by noticing your breathing. Then become aware of the subtle flow of energy within your body and set your intention to increase this flow. Then find a still point in the center of your head and sit in this stillness for 20 – 30 minutes.

Conclusion

"Tomorrow is a new day; begin it well and serenely and with too high a spirit to be encumbered with your old nonsense."

Ralph Waldo Emerson

When we've moved from living a life full of stress and chaos into one filled with peace and calm we've learned how to honor ourselves. We automatically set healthier boundaries, take time to nurture and renew ourselves, and spend time on projects and activities that are inspiring and meaningful to us. This frees up our energy so we can actually be more productive in less time. We also have more time for fun, play and adventure. Living a life of balance may trigger reactions in other people around us. Those who are still caught in the cycle of stress and chaos may be envious or jealous as we breeze through the day accomplishing all of our tasks with ease. Our friends may wonder if we're taking some new form of happy pills, but hopefully they will be awed and inspired to create their own balanced life.

In many ways, creating a balanced lifestyle goes against the grain of western society. Traditionally we have been raised to work hard, struggle through life, give endlessly to others while giving nothing to our self. This has created a society of people externally focused, scattered and lost. Stress, depression, anxiety and addiction are all common ailments associated with this. In changing this trend, we may come up against resistance not only from others, but from our own internal programming as well. This is why it is so important to heighten our awareness of old patterns so we can alter them, weed out limiting beliefs and conditioning that feeds them, and implement new beliefs and behaviors that support us in living balanced, energized lives.

When we forge ahead and do this, we own our freedom and power to choose calm instead of chaos, and we set an example for others to follow. Every path in the forest begins with a trailblazer. Will that trailblazer be you?

Acknowledgements

"I awoke this morning with devout thanksgiving for my dear friends, the old and the new."

Ralph Waldo Emerson

I would first of all like to thank my husband, Richard Best, for his wonderful support and generosity. He has taught me the meaning of gratitude.

This book may not have been written if it were not for the amazing support I received in a Women's Success group. Each of the participants provided encouragement and enthusiasm which motivated me to move forward with my vision. Thank you for being you Diana, Titania, Maureen, Lee and Dee.

An incredible array of teachers and mentors have come into my life over the years contributing to the wisdom in this book.

Sara Baker offered her insightful editing talents and provided the clarity needed for bringing this book to life.

Leah Darling pulled all of the details together in the final editing of the book. Her loving and joyful nature has been an inspiration.

Titania Michniewicz created the beautiful artwork used on the cover and has been an ongoing champion and reminder of the power of my work.

Many friends and family have cheered me on through my adventures with words of wisdom and acts of kindness when I most needed them.

Clients and workshops participants have shown the effectiveness of these tools and I am honored to have shared in their process and journey.

And of course gratitude goes to my dog, Jazzi, who supplied me with much needed amusement and reminded me to take play breaks as often as possible.

About the Author

Gini Grey, founder of Celebrate YourSelf, is a Transformational Coach guiding people to live from their center and create what they want in their life. Gini brings a unique and powerful blend of coaching, counseling and energy healing tools into her Transformational Sessions. An inspiring speaker, Gini gives presentations on a variety of topics including: *Creating Balance, Transforming Stress, Manifest Your Dreams,* and *Energy Awareness.*

Gini has an audio CD titled *Create What You Want In Your Life* and offers a monthly e-zine called *Insights & Inspiration.* Both of these are available on her website at www.ginigrey.com.

Gini lives on beautiful Bowen Island on the west coast of British Columbia, Canada with her husband Richard and their dog Jazzi.

Made in the USA
Lexington, KY
07 October 2011